How To Uncover, Heal & Release Painful Life Experiences

Living a Vocal, Valued and Victorious Life (Vol.1)

Jo Anne Meekins

How To Uncover, Heal & Release Painful Life Experiences

Copyright © 2014 by Jo Anne Meekins.

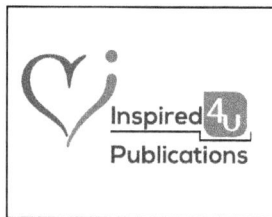

http://www.howtoselfpublishinexcellence.com/

ISBN-13: 978-0692255551

"The wound is the place where the light enters you."

Rumi

Table of Contents

INTRODUCTION...*i*

HOW TO HANDLE THE HIGHS & LOWS OF LIFE *1*

HOW TO HEAL PAINFUL MEMORIES & THE
NEGATIVE EMOTIONS ATTACHED...............................*5*

HOW TO RELEASE THE PAIN THROUGH
FORGIVENESS *9*

HOW TO CONQUER THE INNER-ENEMY...................*13*

POINTS TO REMEMBER DURING SEASONS OF
STRUGGLE...*19*

MY AHA MOMENTS OF SELF-DISCOVERY &
EMOTIONAL HEALING...*23*

HOW I CHANGED FEARFUL AND FALSE
THOUGHTS AND BELIEFS..*33*

HOW I OVERCAME SOME CHALLENGING
TRANSITIONS *49*

ABOUT THE AUTHOR..*61*

INTRODUCTION

The "Living a Vocal, Valued and Victorious Life" three-part series is a collection of learned lessons, experiences and principles that have served to strengthen, mature and improve my life. I openly share my personal experiences and the techniques I've applied over the years because I lived many years as a voiceless, undervalued victim; and I am now purposed to inspire women to keep moving through the highs and lows of living, and to support them in their process with practical and effective tools.

I also speak my truth publically because I believe:

When you tell your truth out loud, you free and empower yourself, heal on deeper levels and give others the permission and power to do the same.

Volume 1, "How To Uncover, Heal & Release Painful Life Experiences," includes tips and techniques on forgiveness, conquering internal conflict, and seasons of struggle. The intention is for you to discover and establish spiritual practices that will facilitate healing, freedom, and peace from the inside out.

HOW TO HANDLE THE HIGHS & LOWS OF LIFE

Most people journey through life experiencing high and low periods. To navigate through these emotional ups and downs, it is helpful to practice techniques that can guide you in ease and elegance through life's see-saw moments.

Embrace the high periods with all your senses, experiencing and classifying what it looks, smells, tastes, feels and sounds like. Capture the experience in your mind, body, soul and spirit such that when anything unlike it shows up and annihilates all traces of your blissful experience, you are able to recall and stand in the high energy experience you previously embraced and captured with your senses.

When the low periods show up in life, and they will because they are necessary for your growth and development, turn within and tap into the power at the core of your being to recall the high energy experience you previously stored. If you have no high period experience to draw from yet, use your senses to imagine what you desire to experience. What would your ideal experience look, smell, taste, feel and sound like? Creatively visualize the experience as if it already is and you are living the desires of your heart in the right now moment.

In addition, practice the following four steps to assist you in your process:

1. **Identify** – Identify what works for you to get you through. Use it consistently, choosing to engage in it instead of wallowing in self-pity or stopping after you feel good for a while.

2. **Journal** – Write it down. Journaling is healing and solidifies what you are striving to accomplish or experience. It also provides a reminder of your struggles, victories and moments of gratitude.

3. **Pray & Meditate** – Be still and know that God is. Turn within and connect to the Source of your supply, strength, wisdom and insight. Listen for

direction and clarity. It is God who makes your way successful.

4. **Decide** – Decide to be the fearfully and wonderfully made purposeful being that God created. Kill off all other options, surrendering all negative thoughts that lie about who you are and what you can do.

Life has a way of shifting our sense of balance from high to low and vice versa. However, there are tools and techniques that can help us maintain a steady course and persevere through challenging transitions.

Use your senses to manifest what you desire, identify what works, journal, pray and decide to be the powerful, authentic, unique spiritual being that you are, with the ability to do all things well.

A lot of our explosive emotional reactions aren't actually a response to the present moment. They're a build-up of all the times we were in a similar dynamic and did not stand up for ourselves, use our voices, or express our emotions. — @haileypaigemagee

HOW TO HEAL PAINFUL MEMORIES & THE NEGATIVE EMOTIONS ATTACHED

Many people survive painful experiences that leave emotional scars, during their lifetime. When painful memories are left unaddressed— ignored, suppressed or buried —they get stuck within our being and block us from experiencing the best most abundant life, divinely purposed and planned by God.

Now is the time to heal any painful memories and the negative emotions attached! The following four suggestions will help you begin the process to break any unaddressed emotional chains that may be blocking your blessings:

1. **Get in the flow of God's will** – It is God's will for you to prosper in every way and be in good health. Present your body to God and renew your mind for transformation through the promises and guidance of God's word. Unresolved issues can manifest in the body as illness. Read, believe and receive your inheritance of healing and wholeness.

2. **Set the intention** – Determine to heal any memories that make you cringe, cry, or keep secret and bound in pain and shame. Make the decision to be free and unblock the move of God in your life.

3. **Ask and allow God** – Seek God to reveal and guide you on what needs to be healed. Be still and know you are safe in God. Listen for the answer and instruction. Allow God to strengthen and reward you through the healing process.

4. **Release the pain** – Break the emotional chain and remove its power by:
- Journaling about everything and everyone who comes forth, regarding the memory.
- Speak it out loud.
- Be more loving of self in spite of poor choices.
- Forgive all involved, including yourself.

- Thank God for resurrecting the memory to be healed.

- Reframe it to an ideal outcome, associating individual colors that come to mind with the new memory experience.

- Mentally bathe yourself repeatedly in those colors one at a time, and then combine the colors into a molecule and move it through your entire body from the crown of your head, down and out through the soles of your feet.

Do the necessary work to reap the rewards of freedom, empowerment and abundance. When you heal the painful memories in your life, you unblock and release an increase of peace, joy, love for self and others, gratitude, praise and intimacy with God.

Also, consider affirming Iyanla Vanzant's lesson of ego and healing (dominate thought- I'm so ashamed!) from "Faith in the Valley," page 30:

DEAR SELF,

Guilt says,
"There is something wrong with what I have done."

Shame says,
"There is something wrong with me."

You can eliminate guilt by making amends for what you have done.

You cannot eliminate shame until you know and believe,
"All that God is, I Am."

God is truth, mercy, wisdom, strength, forgiveness, peace, order, justice and love.

What have you got to be ashamed of?

God is not ashamed of me. Neither am I.

HOW TO RELEASE THE PAIN THROUGH FORGIVENESS

Forgiveness liberates you from the pain and trauma of your past, present and future experiences, which is more to your benefit than to the person you are choosing to forgive. It is all about you making a choice to be free from the bondage of holding onto hurts that hinder your progress and prosperity. Unforgiveness will only serve to block your blessings, generate pain and manifest illness.

"For if you forgive other people when they sin against you, your heavenly Father will also forgive you. But if you do not forgive others their sins, your Father will not forgive your sins." (Matthew 6:14-15)

I offer the following forgiveness affirmation,

technique, and prayer to assist you in your process of forgiveness:

1. **Affirmation** – Unblock your flow by affirming:

   "All that has offended me, I forgive. Within and without, I forgive. Things past, things present, things future, I forgive. I forgive everything and everybody who can possibly need forgiveness in my past and present. I forgive positively everyone. I am free, and all others are free too. All things are cleared up between us, now and forever." ~ Catherine Ponder

2. **Technique** – Forgiveness Diet: Ask Spirit to bring to mind all people and situations you need to forgive, including yourself, and do the following exercise for seven consecutive days:

   • Before Noon, write 35 times: "I, (your name), forgive (name of person) totally and unconditionally." (If more than one name comes up just list them all in one sentence, do not write the statement 35 times for each person individually).

- <u>Before Midnight</u>, write 35 times: "I, (your name), forgive myself totally and unconditionally. I am free to move on to wholeness and completion."

NOTE: If you miss a day or time, you must start the consecutive seven day cycle over. This technique is an abridged version based on Iyanla Vanzant's exercise in "Tapping The Power Within."

---

3. **Prayer** – "Soul Secrets when it's hard to forgive" by Bishop T.D. Jakes (Thomas Nelson-Holy Bible, Woman Thou Art Loosed Edition, pg. 1079)

"Lord, there is nothing harder than trying to forgive when you've been desperately wounded. It's worse when the offenders show no remorse, but gloat over the pain they have brought to your life. And that's where I am. I do not want to forgive.

"But I know enough to understand that the command of Your Holy Word is forgiveness– no matter what. You have not given me an option.

"Help me to realize that unforgiveness can kill my

friendships, my joy, even my body. So Lord, I am choosing today to forgive all those who have stolen from me, all who have broken my heart, all who have wounded my body or my soul, all who have haunted me for years. In the name of Jesus, I forgive.

"Thank You, Lord, for strength to walk out this forgiveness in my life. Thank You for using it as a testimony to the power of Your love. And thank You that, as I choose to forgive moment by moment, the feelings will follow."

Choose to release your pain through forgiveness, using affirmations, techniques and prayer to support you on your journey toward increased love, joy, peace, abundance, freedom and wholeness.

Love, forgiveness and gratitude are the keys to victorious living!

HOW TO CONQUER THE INNER-ENEMY

When the Enemy Is the Inner Me...

Has your life's journey been easy and effortless or painful and complicated?

It is often easier and more comfortable to look outside of ourselves for the causes of our circumstances and situations when in reality, the answer and enemy is usually found within. The solution to conquering the enemy begins with us and the continual inner-work that is essential for our personal well-being, healing, wholeness and successful living.

If you are not experiencing the life you want to

live or find yourself getting in your own way for fear of failure or success, then the following six steps may be beneficial for you to consider and implement in a spiritual practice:

1. **Identify and clearly define what you truly desire to experience**. Having a goal to focus your energy towards makes it easier to visualize, determine and plan the action steps necessary for attainment.

"Friends, don't get me wrong: By no means do I count myself an expert in all of this, but I've got my eye on the goal, where God is beckoning us onward– to Jesus. I'm off and running, and I'm not turning back." (Philippians 3:13-14)

2. **Come into alignment with what God wills for your life**. Be open for God's will to be done in your life as it is in heaven. Spend time with God to help you know Him and understand His word, His will, and yourself. You will be better able to determine what God wills for you and align your will and desires to His.

"This, then, is how you should pray: 'Our Father in heaven, hallowed be your name, your kingdom come, your will be done on earth as it is in heaven." (Matthew 6:9-10)

3. **Meditate and seek divine revelation and guidance.** Sit quietly, breathe deeply, release the head chatter and focus on your heart center. Ask Spirit how you are not showing up for yourself, what your fears are, how you are blocking your way, and how to address what comes present for you. Be open, honest and willing to go deep beneath the surface, back to when the issues originated and the first experiences occurred, even into childhood.

"In the same way, the Spirit helps us in our weakness. We do not know what we ought to pray for, but the Spirit himself intercedes for us with groans that words cannot express. And he who searches our hearts knows the mind of the Spirit, because the Spirit intercedes for the saints in accordance with God's will." (Romans 8:26-27)

4. **Take every thought captive.** Filter your thoughts and cancel, counter and resist every thought that is negative and destructive or does not serve you or your vision.

"We demolish arguments and every pretension that sets itself up against the knowledge of God, and we take captive every thought to make it obedient to Christ." (2 Corinthians 10:5)

5. **Engage in and continue the process.** There are lessons to be learned and issues to be healed on

deeper levels; so just when you think you've passed a test or learned a lesson, you may find yourself going through a similar experience. Its ok, God wants to strengthen and deepen your faith in that area and move you forward into your divine destiny.

"Consider it pure joy, my brothers, whenever you face trials of many kinds, because you know that the testing of your faith develops perseverance. Perseverance must finish its work so that you may be mature and complete, not lacking anything."
(James 1:2-4)

6. **Ask for support when necessary**. You don't have to figure it out on your own. Ask for what you need from those who are where you want to go and doing what you want to do. Avail yourself to healing and growth opportunities through entities such as group or individual coaching, counseling, spiritual communities, healing circles and workshops.

"Ask and it will be given to you; seek and you will find; knock and the door will be opened to you. For everyone who asks receives; he who seeks finds; and to him who knocks, the door will be opened." (Matthew 7:7-8)

The combination of our life experiences contribute to our mental and emotional make up, often creating issues that need to be explored, healed and conquered. When the state of our inner-being causes us to operate as the enemy in self-destructive ways or shut down and not function, we need to seek out and implement ways that assist us in moving forward in purpose, divine alignment, growth, healing, transformation, confidence and victory, as indicated in the steps above.

Identifying the pattern is awareness;
*choosing **not** to repeat the cycle is growth.*

Billy Chapata

POINTS TO REMEMBER DURING SEASONS OF STRUGGLE

Everyone will experience challenging times during some point in their life if they keep living. Seasons of struggle are necessary for us to mature and grow in faith and we are to count it pure joy. However, going through does not always feel good and can cause us to lose perspective, so I offer the following five points to remember during those inevitable seasons of struggle.

1. **Focus on the positive** – Take every thought captive, releasing the negative and intentionally meditating on the positive uplifting thoughts that are true.

2. **Hold on till your breakthrough** – Jacob

wrestled with the angel until the angel blessed him. The blessing is often two steps past giving up, so don't quit in the midst of the struggle. Hold on, learn the lesson and obtain your victory.

3. **God is keeping you** – God is a present help and will preserve you from all evil. He promises to never leave nor forsake you.

4. **God is able** – There is nothing too hard for God and He is faithful to do what He promised. He spoke the world into existence and brought forth our redemption through a virgin birth. He is the same yesterday, today and forever.

5. **Read and remember** – Read the Word, stand on God's promises and remember what He has already done to bless your life and bring you through. Count your blessings and review your victories.

It is not what we experience in life that matters, but how we endure and overcome that adds meaning to our lives and others. Remember to stay positive, hold onto your faith, and read God's word. God is able and will help you to persevere with joy and thanksgiving, please Him, and sow seeds to receive an abundant harvest when your season of struggle is over.

*"Nothing ever goes away until it has taught us
what we need to know."*

Pema Chödrön

PERSONAL EXPERIENCES OF
ENLIGHTENMENT, HEALING
AND VICTORY

MY AHA MOMENTS OF SELF-DISCOVERY & EMOTIONAL HEALING

The Plan and the Purpose...

Oprah Winfrey often inquired about the defining "aha" moments in a guest's life when they had journeyed through troubling life experiences. Those moments of clarity usually summarized the lessons learned and revealed the origin of the problems that hindered the people from progressing in their lives. The "aha" awareness allowed them to address the issues, make changes and discover a different path when necessary.

In my continued journey toward self-discovery, healing and wholeness, I uncovered some deep-seated trust issues while working through the meditation assignments of a coaching program I joined in 2010.

Meditation is to engage in contemplation or reflection through various styles and techniques. I believe anyone can benefit from the practice of meditation if they set a sincere intention, breathe deeply, call for God's insight and guidance, and stay in the moment with whatever shows up.

For me, during my meditation sessions, I found that I had to keep both feet firmly planted on the floor because I sometimes experienced the desire to not want to sit in the emotions that were coming up. Planting my feet helps me stay grounded in the moment even now.

The purpose of my meditation journey was to define the authentic ideal life that I wanted to create and remove anything that blocked, limited or inhibited the natural flow of abundance that I am. Assisting me on that journey was Rev. Valerie Love, Coach and Mentor of The Science of Getting Rich program. I joined the program because I recognized that I had some long standing issues around money which were a concern because I am an author with books to sell, and I desire financial freedom and the ability to work from home in full-time entrepreneurial ministry. Knowing that I couldn't get to the next level on my own, I decided to take action toward fulfilling my dreams in that now moment. If not now, when?

In less than a month of taking the step, I was surprised by the awareness that "lack of trust" was the underlying factor in many issues that started long ago. These issues have affected me throughout my life, including my present 33 year relationship with God (my true Source and Supply).

Defining the Moments...

During my meditations, I saw myself at different ages from toddler to adulthood. I care-fronted resurfacing issues that include abandonment, insecurity, unworthiness, betrayal, sexual assault, double-mindedness and fear of rejection. I also wrote letters of LOVE and FORGIVENESS to myself at those ages and have identified defining moments that crystallized in my consciousness. These defining moments are being dismantled and released in order to unblock the flow of money, move forward, and experience my divine inheritance. I invite you into my journey as I share the following transparent moments of my life:

AGE 11: I was scheduled to have eye surgery on my "lazy" left eye only (my right eye was 20/20). When I was wheeled into surgery and *before* my mother arrived at the hospital, the intern who performed the surgery stated that he was going to operate on both eyes to make it easier for my recovery. When my mother arrived, she was shocked and livid to see my right eye also operated on without her presence or permission. However, we never received justice or compensation because we didn't have money for a lawyer and had to deal with Legal Aid. The hospital and doctors stood behind their intern's decision, stating that he did a wonderful job, and the Legal Aid Lawyer wouldn't pursue the case.

My 11 year old self felt vulnerable and unprotected. Through that defining moment, I decided that:

- Lack of money = Loss of rights and no protection.

- If my family had money, I would have been valued and defended.

AGE 17: During the end of my first semester in

college, I had the opportunity to stay in the dorms over the summer and regroup from the traumas of that year. However, my mother refused to pay the dorm fee and insisted that I come home because I had really botched up my first semester. It had been a challenging year for me being ill-equipped to manage my emotions around my first experience in the loss of a loved one (my grandfather, whose home I was raised in); my boyfriend's arrest for assault in a provoked fight; and the rape, my first sexual penetration. At one point, I thought I would lose my mind, but I survived it all and was determined to press forward and do better. Mom's refusal deflated my hope like a torpedo bursting a Good Year Blimp-size balloon. Thank God for Grandma, who provided the summer dorm fee because she knew that home would not be the best environment for me at the time.

My 17 year old self felt disappointed in my mom's response and decided in that defining moment that:

- When I need money, I have to depend on the discretion of others no matter how important or beneficial the need is to me.

- Even when I work hard to overcome trials and poor choices, learn the lessons and make amends, I don't deserve a second chance and will not receive the support from the people I expect or desire the most.

- Everyone, especially family and friends, will not celebrate or support my "aha" moments, deliverance, victories or second chances.

AGE 17: During the <u>2nd semester</u> of that first year, my roommate was spring cleaning and tricked my boyfriend to unknowingly throw out several pairs of my shoes, which were stored in a black plastic bag. She also allowed the perpetrator, who raped me, into our room and my bed while I was in a drunken sleep (first semester, see YouTube channel to hear my "One Billion Rising: I Rise 4 U" story and see article link). I observed that she was a single mother of 3-boys, older than me, not considered attractive or popular, and had non-existing support and limited funds. Whereas, my mom and grandparents made sure I had all I needed in material possessions.

My 17 year old self decided in that defining moment of the shoes (because it took me 20 years to deal with the rape) that:

- People will pretend to be my friend while plotting evil and devious schemes behind my back when they are jealous and perceive me to be more affluent then them.

- Having money or the appearance of such will cause people to hate me.

- When you have money, you can't trust people's motives for liking you.

So as you can see by my defining moments, I had conflicting emotions and beliefs around money buried in my subconscious that needed be addressed.

Revelations, Gratitude and Affirmations...

For as long as I could remember, I desired and sought to obtain love, peace, security, understanding and trust from other people. I have since learned on a deeper level that I have to be those things for myself before I can attract or experience them from another. So I committed to go within and give to my younger selves all that was perceived as lacking while growing up. I now know that I already possess everything I need or desire. I am complete in God.

NOTE: During an entire week of writing letters to my younger self, showering her with love and asking forgiveness for not knowing how to take better care of her at the time, it didn't dawn on me until day 7 that I had not forgiven her on paper or within for some of the choices and behaviors of our past. It was indeed an AHA Moment that made me smile and shine light in my heart and soul, as I corrected that oversight.

I praise God that I am gaining a better understanding of who I am and what I desire. As I work through my trust issues, money is becoming less of a consideration in making decisions and my trust in God is being strengthened. I am also learning to embrace *being* instead of expending a lot of time and energy in *doing*. When I am simply *being*, I discover the authentic desire of what I am seeking to create. When I am busy *doing*, I find that I make decisions to please others or get distracted by information overload and business related things that are not necessarily the best thing for me. I believe the monies will show up when I focus my energies on being the best inspirational writer and encourager that God has called, planned and purposed me to be.

Science of Getting Rich Reminders…

- Wealth is not something I have to make happen.

- Abundance is not something I have to get.

- I am ALREADY abundant.

- I am ALREADY wealthy.

- I was created so by the Divine.

My only work is to remove anything that blocks, limits, or inhibits the natural flow of abundance that I am.

My only work is to ALLOW abundance to manifest in my bank accounts and pockets.

"In the process of letting go you will lose many things from the past. But you will find yourself."

Deepak Chopra

HOW I CHANGED FEARFUL AND FALSE THOUGHTS AND BELIEFS

Erroneous Beliefs and Revelations...

Inner work is a critical component of the journey toward healing and wholeness. Without the resolve to confront and work through personal issues, I would venture to say that abundance and successful authentic living will always be just beyond reach for some and impossible for others. How can a person know self, love self or be self without self-examination and a determination to address past memories and experiences that may have caused error thinking in their consciousness?

Without confronting the issues and learning the lessons, we are doomed to repeat patterns that we don't understand or may not be aware of. We risk blocking the abundant life that Christ came for us to have because when we don't face ourselves, we can't learn our lessons, heal or forgive our hurts and move forward in freedom. However, there are ways that we can change negative and fearful thoughts, and erroneous beliefs.

In my ongoing process of working through my defining moments and trust issues, I discovered that the following false beliefs had also crystallized in my consciousness:

- What I desire is not as important as the desires of others.

- Other people's needs outweigh my wants.

- My money should be spent for the needs of others before my own.

- In order to make ends meet, I will have to compromise my heart's desire and possibly sleep with the enemy.

- When I don't have sufficient income, I have to settle for what I don't really want to experience.

- If I don't go along with the general

consensus, it will be costly and will upset and hurt people.

In working through my defining moments and trust issues, I asked my younger self what she would like and what would make her feel better. She asked for me to:

- Be totally satisfied and fulfilled in God, and no longer seek that fulfillment outside of my godly-self.

- Learn how to wait right and just do what needs to be done.

- No longer entertain, for even a fleeting moment, unequal yoking or inappropriate advances.

- Do things differently than in the past.

- Be true to myself, obedient to Spirit, and trusting of God in all, for all and through all things.

Because Christ lives, I can face tomorrow...

Confession & Forgiveness...

Also in working through my defining moments and trust issues, I needed to acknowledge and confess the constant **FEAR of living life and**

facing the future from childhood through adulthood. That fear was overshadowed and assuaged by a greater fear of the alternative–vegetating into nowhere and nothingness. Even though I pressed forward in life, I did so in great fear for the first half of my life. And **I was never fully committed to living**. I was always more comfortable and at peace with the notion of God taking me whenever He wanted. I actually preferred it sooner than later because life felt too hard. I was eager to escape, inwardly running away from myself, confrontation and living life in general.

This confession also surfaced when my inner child expressed what she needed from me in order to feel better.

She wanted me to commit to:

- Live! and no longer entertain the thought of going home to glory.
- Stop running and stand in the here and now, staying on this side of heaven until my work is done and God calls me home.
- Stop being ready to go just because life is a struggle.

She would feel better if:

- I truly trusted and believed that God is my

Source, Supply and Support, and that I already have everything I need.

- From this day forth, I go forward expectant of receiving the desires of my heart and believe without doubt that they have already been granted; God has perfected what concerns me; and God has worked all things together for my good.

My younger self and I forgive each other and ourselves for the pain of the past and any poor choices of the present, submitting ourselves to God for the future. Our times are in His hands and He has given us a prosperous plan, hope and future.

Commitment...

I commit to "Act As If!" Act like I know. Walk in it; talk in it; think in it; be in it. It = My abundance, my natural divine state created so by the Divine:

- I am wealthy.
- I am rich.
- I am abundant.
- I am fearfully and wonderfully made.

I commit to be determined and steadfast; and not compromise or settle anymore.

I commit to walk worthy, talk worthy, and be worthy– trustworthy.

I commit to stand in the power and anointing of my Highest Most Holy Self, which is "Fearless Unconditional Love" of God, of myself and of others.

I commit to LIVE in the present, right now moments of my life!

HOW SPIRITUAL JOURNALING HEALED MY FATHER-DAUGHTER ISSUES AFTER HIS DEATH

Spiritual Journaling Benefits & Steps...

Spiritual Journaling helped me heal issues of guilt and unforgiveness concerning my father after he died. It is a resourceful tool, which contains several techniques that can be instrumental in disciplining you to discover and document your spiritual journey. Keeping a history of God's faithful presence throughout your life can serve as a source of encouragement during personal reflection and in sharing with others. It can also become the foundation of your memoirs or testimony as a legacy for generations following.

The Dialogue method will allow you to address people, projects, events, ideas, your body and inner realities, where guilt, pain or questions emerge. The steps include: 1) Recall and write out the whole situation in great detail; 2) Offer the situation to God in prayer; and 3) Begin the dialogue regarding the details. "In doing so, you will often receive insight as to what is required in the present to defuse (or grow beyond) the past." (Spiritual Journaling: Recording Your Journey Toward God by Richard Peace).

In 2005, I attended a Spiritual Journaling class. The use of Richard Peace's book yielded surprising results in helping me to heal, on a deeper level, some age old issues that were still very present within me. Practicing the Dialogue technique proved to be the most challenging and revealing experiences of the class. I share my experience of healing, forgiveness and hope, with the prayerful intention to facilitate healing in those of you with a similar circumstance and inspire all of you to explore the practice of spiritual journaling and incorporate it into your own process of self-discovery.

The Acknowledgment…

I acknowledged in my latter years that my heart's desire and passion in life, since about age 15, was that I yearned for a soul mate to love with my whole heart. Someone who understood me and loved me inside and out, from the imperfect outer shell to the depth of my being.

For too many years, I remained in a holding pattern, wondering if I would ever get the opportunity to release the abundance of love I possessed. A love that used to seem so intense it overwhelmed me when I pondered the possibility of releasing it within the confines of the divine relationship I long awaited. I came to believe that the desire stemmed from the following two childhood factors:

1. Although I was acquainted with many people growing up and participated in social activities, I was always a loner at heart; and a deep thinker, who often felt misunderstood at the core, and who was more comfortable at home reading a book, watching TV, or taking a nap.

2. I never had a civil relationship with my biological father during his lifetime; in fact, our interactions were basically non-existent.

Dialogue with my Biological Father...

Me: Father, I'm sorry for my behavior during most of your life. I didn't know how to do it different at the time and I was operating out of a child's perception of distorted facts. I guess I took after mommy with my attitude. Remember, everything was either black or white with no shades of gray in between.

Father: Jo Anne, why were you so cold and distant every time I tried reconnecting with you? We never talked.

Me: Father, I believed that you had abandoned your children because you were mad at mommy; and I felt that if you really loved us, you would have maintained your responsibilities. I felt like you wronged us, so I cut you off emotionally. I apologize for never treating you with love (as far as I can remember) and I repent for not being spiritually mature enough to seek you out and share my faith after I received the Lord.

Father: Jo Anne, I can't say that I wasn't saddened and hurt by your treatment of me, but I am thankful that you eventually became civil. You did stop referring to me by my last name only and you stopped looking at me with disgust and contempt. I never held it against you; I named you and have always loved you.

Me: Thank you, Father, and forgive me for not sharing my hope with you when you were at your lowest. I regret the wasted years of never knowing you as a person or a father. I did eventually come to realize that I was wrong about you and had acquired some of your attributes, like your good-natured personality, dancing ability and sense of humor. I think that our lack of relationship and understanding have been the seedling for my heart's desire. I love you Father and hope to rejoice with you on the other side.

Dialogue with GOD, my Heavenly Daddy...

GOD: My daughter. *Yes Daddy.* I have already forgiven you for that and it is time for you to release it completely. *I know Daddy, but–* JO ANNE! I know you are fearful that your father died in his sin and you blame yourself for not being a witness.

Me: Yes Daddy, I don't even know exactly when or where he died or what he died from, but I know he wasn't doing well and that his life and his choices had taken a toll on his health and his physical body.

GOD: Let it go my daughter, it is what it is. Release the past in order to be completely healed and embrace your future. You have repented and are forgiven. His soul is in My hands and I will render the judgment of lives lived. Learn your lessons and move on.

Me: Daddy, will I ever get this relationship thing right?

GOD: Baby Girl, when and only when your relationship is right with me and I AM enough for you, will you be able to experience that which you desire most. Until then, you are not ready. I understand the root and intensity of your desire, but to obtain it outside of me can destroy you. As a child, you were an old soul with questions and fears about life that no one took the time to listen to or could answer for you. You desired someone who would love and care for you and walk through this journey of life with you. You knew nothing of me at the time, but I was always the answer to those fears and questions and I AM the fulfillment of that desire.

Me: Daddy, I know that to be true in my head and in my heart of hearts, but you know that it has been a longstanding issue with us, and my own personal stronghold, to experience your love in the flesh. That's how I ended up in my first marriage (and I say first because it is my desire that I will have a second chance).

GOD: No daughter, you ended up in your first marriage because of disobedience. You made your own decision and didn't listen or WAIT on Me, then you got scared and didn't know what to do and went ahead because you didn't talk to ME! To endure 11 years, you prayed for a special love and plenty of grace, but you didn't repent until 10 years had passed. By then, you were lonelier married than you had been single, and were dying a slow spiritual and emotional death. And as for a second chance, only if and when you are ready.

Me: Daddy, what do I need to do in preparation?

GOD: Yield precious one. Give Me your whole heart, especially the part reserved for your soul mate. Enter into the center of My will. When you give up total control, I can complete the good work I've begun in you. Accept my will, even if it means to live single in a life of service. Open your heart and let me pour the fullness of Me into you. My love will allow you to love me right and true, and help you desire what I want for you.

Me: Thank you, Daddy, all that You say I will do. I know that Your will for my life is far better than anything I can want or orchestrate for myself. I have learned and truly believe that it is better to live a full life alone than to live a life with someone and be lonely. I pray your kingdom come in my life.

GOD: Dear heart, in doing so, you will receive a glorious inheritance and I will reward your humble obedience, exceedingly abundantly above all that you ask or think.

Me: Let it be so and so it is! In Jesus' name, amen.

The Healing…

After years of not learning the lesson, failed tests, and repeating the same class on the topic of "Love, Lust and Compromise vs. God: Enduring Love, Meeting Every Need," breakthrough finally occurred. I learned to separate myself, set boundaries, shut out distractions and the input of others, and develop a direct intimate connection to the Source and Creator of all things.

How could I have given or received love without knowing and experiencing the true, pure love of God, who is LOVE! For the first time in my life, I am really in love. I thought I was three times before, but now I know that was just practice love– a yearning little girl's love, not fully developed.

Pentecost is real; the Comforter has come and is the same yesterday, today and forever. I am empowered and delivered through the outpouring of the Holy Spirit. I walk in confident victory by faith, unto the full manifestation of my deliverance.

Do I still desire a committed physical relationship? Yes, but only if God wills it. And now that I am assured I will not self-destruct without it, nor settle for less receiving it, I no longer desire to look or wait around for love. I have entered into an exclusive relationship with Love, who is alive within me. I am validated everyday by a new level of intimacy beyond what I could ask or think. My God, El Shaddai, is more than enough, speaking ceaseless revelations through His word and inspiring unlimited constant creativity within me. If or when it is time, the love I desire will find me being about my heavenly Father's business.

"But seek first the kingdom of God and His righteousness, and all these things shall be added to you." (Matthew 6:33)

To forgive is to set a prisoner free and discover that the prisoner was you.

Lewis B. Smedes

HOW I OVERCAME SOME CHALLENGING TRANSITIONS

Experiencing A Major Transition...

The year was 1999: two years after leaving an 11 year marriage and my residential house of 6 years. In August 1997, I had returned to my childhood home to stay with my mom for a season of emotional healing and renewal, which lasted till February 2003 (much longer than I had intended). Although grateful for an alternative place to live, the dilapidated environment of leaking bathroom pipes, a crumbling kitchen ceiling, broken windows, and peeling paint inside and outside of the house, generated feelings of shame in my new living conditions and resentment at giving up my house with its renovated bathroom and structural soundness. However, I learned to thankfully focus on the blessings of heat and hot water and not fester on my displeasure at bathing in a bucket placed in the tub to circumvent faulty plumbing and diminish water from leaking into the kitchen.

"For I have learned to be content whatever the circumstances. I know what it is to be in need and I know what it is to have plenty. I have learned the secret of being content in any and every situation, whether well fed or hungry, whether living in plenty or in want." (Philippians 4:11-12)

Faith is the first source of survival during transitions of hardship in my life. I always believed that in spite of limited finances and no visible resources, circumstances would improve for me and my mother.

A Faith Confession…

At the time, I was working as Assistant Program Manager for Rockaway Vendor Housekeeping Services until February 1999 when the bus I was traveling to work on stopped short to avoid hitting a car that had run a stop sign. I was thrown from my seat in the back and slammed face down into the floor a few feet away from the bus driver. This accident resulted in facial contusions, bulging discs in my back, degenerative nerve damage in my neck, and a groin hernia that had to be surgically repaired.

I also suffered from severe cash-flow depletion due to my personal ignorance regarding such matters and my poor choice in counsel. I never received lost wages, ended up paying cab fare to go to and from physical therapy, and my disability check was 2/3 less than my usual pay. I was in pain, stressed-out, frustrated, uncertain, insecure and afraid. Not prone to being ill for long periods of time, I didn't understand what was happening to my body, how this turn of events was going to unfold, or how long it would last. Ironically, since 1997 I had repeatedly told co-workers, friends, and church advisors, "I don't know when or how, but I will not be at my job long. By my 40th birthday in 2000, I want to be doing my reason for being." And in 1998, I had also confessed a desire to move into full-time ministry.

"We can make our plans, but the Lord determines our steps."
(Proverbs 16:9)

Discipline is the second source of survival during transitions of hardship in my life. I needed to establish some practices that would serve as action steps toward the manifestation of my heart's desire.

Practicing Disciplines...

Four months into the disability leave, I determined to maximize my time at home if I was going to be serious about my writing. I purchased the 1999 Writer's Market and dug out copies of my old writing magazine subscriptions and identified some poetry contests. Over the next several months to a year, I submitted old and newly created poems for requested themes by the specified deadlines; joined some book clubs, and spiritual and writing organizations (e.g., volunteering with the National Writers Union and becoming a delegate); subscribed to writing magazines; and also completed and copyrighted a poetry manuscript (the first draft of On Solid Ground: Inspirational Poetry For All Occasions).

My disability benefits maxed out in September 1999 and I still needed four more weeks just to heal from the hernia surgery in addition to the nerve damage in my neck. During this time, my faith-walk kicked up a notch as I began to insert my name in the appropriate places of scriptures that applied to my present situations and the situations that I desired to experience. I declared them out loud in my conversations and in my prayers and praise, making my way by speaking them into existence. I listened to and studied God's promises for me until they became rooted in my spirit and I could easily and quickly counter attacks of doubt and depression with positive affirmations and scriptural confessions of faith.

"In the sight of God in Whom he believed, Who gives life to the dead and speaks of the nonexistent things that [He has foretold and promised] as if they [already] existed." (Romans 4:17b)

Perseverance is the third source of survival during transitions of hardship in my life. I had to keep believing and striving forward in spite of difficulties, opposition and discouragement.

Striving To Persevere…

The year 2000 was uneventful and financially lean, stirring up constant doubts that caused me to second-guess myself and God's direction for my life. It was a challenge to stay focused, disciplined, obedient, creative and consistent; and to not give up, confidently believing that God would do what He said in spite of how I felt or what it looked like. Although one of my poems was published in a poetry anthology, I wasn't winning any contests; and in December 1999, I chose to resign from the company I had worked 13 years with because of 1) the pressure to return before I was physically ready; 2) the knowledge that my heart wasn't in it anymore; and 3) the belief that God had a greater plan and purpose for me.

To keep my phone on and pay for basic personal items, I was encouraged to dust off my Express Yourself Creations home-based business and provide some writing services. I framed and sold a couple of the poems from my manuscript; wrote and framed a personalized tribute for a friend's mother; and did some editing for a friend and business associate. I also received some unexpected monetary gifts from people that I had been a blessing to as I was able throughout the years.

"Brethren, I do not count myself to have apprehended; but one thing I do, forgetting those things which are behind and reaching forward to those things which are ahead, I press toward the goal for the prize of the upward call of God in Christ Jesus." (Philippians 3:13-14)

Seizing Opportunity is the fourth source of survival during transitions of hardship in my life. I stayed open to and listened out for alternative income sources.

Seizing Opportunity...

By the start of 2001, I began looking into the job market again. A friend told me that Con Edison was hiring, so I took the test and started the eight-week paid Customer Service training in March 2001. Although I had no desire to answer phones, I enjoyed the weekly paycheck and the psychology of the training course. I was the top student in my class. After the last day of training in May 2001, on the same day that I aced the final exam, I was a passenger in another motor vehicle accident. Dazed and gripped by the feeling of déjà vu and the aggravation of my prior injuries, I was strapped to a board, transported to the hospital, treated and released.

I followed the leading of my inner spirit regarding the selection of legal counsel and trusted God to provide, which was easier to do this time around with no health coverage and meager finances. I experienced God's guidance and favor from beginning to end and gracefully eased through the process, unlike the first accident when I reacted to the situation in fear and ignorant vulnerability. And when Con Edison terminated me according to policy, *"for being out more than ten days"* due to the car accident, I was relieved that I wouldn't have to deal with self-pressure or employer harassment to return to work before I was truly ready. I survived off of lost wages and related expenses that were paid expeditiously.

In 2002, I reconnected with a childhood friend who was working at the New York Christian Times (NYCT) in Brooklyn. She got me an interview with the publisher and I consented to write two unpaid articles on assignment in April (a Good Friday Service) and May (a Friendship Day Program), both published in their respective 2002 editions of the paper. In July 2002, I was hired at NYCT as Office Administrator with a weekly stipend and no benefits. I gained more experience with the opportunity to interview and write an article on an advertiser, businesswoman Cynthia Boone, that was published twice in subsequent editions.

"A gift opens the way and ushers the giver into the presence of the great." (Proverbs 18:16)

Continuing Education is the fifth source of survival during transitions of hardship in my life. I satisfied the need to increase my marketability by sharpening my knowledge in my desired area of expertise.

Continuing My Education…

In September 2001, I was able to start classes toward a certificate in Communication Skills at NYU School of Continuing and Professional Studies through the lost wages from the second accident. The case was settled within six months, enabling me to pay the required tuition and complete the certificate program in the fall of 2002. Both settlements were much less than expected and the settlement for the first accident took so long, I can't even remember when I received it. Yet, I was grateful that the monies allowed me to help my mom, educate myself and take care of some necessities.

I was laid off from NYCT after the holidays in December 2002 and a friend told me about a free Adult Occupational Training Program that had sites in each borough. I applied for and began the Computerized Office Technology certificate course at the Queens Adult Learning Center in Long Island City. I became ill, soon after I started classes, with a severe case of bronchitis from staying in my mom's house for three days with no heat when the boiler broke in February 2003. I moved in with my spiritual mom for a season, depleted the remainder of my finances to pay for medicine and emergency room costs, and then applied for Public Assistance (PA) to pay rent and basic needs. I was told that I had to report to a program to qualify for benefits, but thank God for favor because the PA program was in the same building as the certificate program; and my PA case manager allowed me to sign in each day with her and then go continue my training classes. Glory to God, in spite of being ill and missing classes, I was the top student again!

In April 2003, I received a phone message to call and schedule an interview for a Procedure Writer position at Healthfirst, Inc. I was shocked and afraid because I had never applied to that company and to this day I'm not sure if my NYCT childhood friend, who also worked at Healthfirst, floated my resume or if they found my resume on Monster.com or Careerbuilders.com. I also had some insecurities about my writing abilities and this potential move into the corporate arena; however, I could not pass up what I deemed to be a God-orchestrated opportunity. Subsequently, I was referred to the Dress For Success organization, where I was able to get free business attire that included the power suit I wore for the interview.

In May 2003, I had to end the training program early because my new position at Healthfirst started on the same day I was supposed to start a job working for a welfare check. The position at Healthfirst was newly created and filled by me after being previously serviced by an outside consultant. God is good all the time and His timing is awesome! Even though I was unable to finish the Microsoft Access portion of the training or go to the June graduation ceremony, I still received my certificate; and remained an employee of Healthfirst as their Policies and Procedures Writer until I resigned on July 30, 2010 to pursue my soul purpose and ministry vision full time.

"Study and be eager and do your utmost to present yourself to God approved (tested by trial), a workman who has no cause to be ashamed, correctly analyzing and accurately dividing [rightly handling and skillfully teaching] the Word of Truth. (2 Timothy 2:15)

Faith, Discipline, Perseverance, Seizing Opportunity, and Continuing Education are the sources of survival during transitions of hardship in my life that lead from famine to fruitfulness.

POST SCRIPT:

Putting this collection of my articles together to support and encourage others has served to uplift me with reminders of God's faithfulness and steps of what to do during seasons of struggle. It is also interesting to re-experience the faith walk challenges that come with living on purpose, as I chose to do when I resigned from my two major jobs in 1999 and 2010.

As I read this last chapter and complete this first volume of "Living a Vocal, Valued and Victorious Life," I am reminded that I am more than a conqueror, who serves a good God that can do anything but fail! I am grateful and expectant as I continue to obey God's direction to:

"Write down clearly on tablets what I reveal to you, so that it can be read at a glance." (Habakkuk 2:2)

ABOUT THE AUTHOR

Jo Anne Meekins is the founder of Inspired 4 U Publications and a publisher, poet, coach, and author of nine books as of 2022. She provides editing, formatting, and publishing services to authors; and empowers them how to publish in excellence, maintaining total control of their product, using the Kindle Direct Publishing (KDP) platform, even if they are technology challenged.

You can contact Jo Anne for comments and inquiries about her books and services via her website at —
http://www.howtoselfpublishinexcellence.com.

* * *

More Books by Author Jo Anne Meekins

1. On Solid Ground: Inspirational Poetry For All Occasions (2nd Edition)

2 Relationship Seasons of Love (Poetry)

3. How to Protect Yourself From 'Pretend' Friend Requests & Email Scams

4. For Such A Time As This (Poetry)

5. How to Self-Publish in Excellence within 10-Days: A step-by-step guide to self-publishing via CreateSpace

3-VOLUME SERIES – Living a Vocal, Valued and Victorious Life:

6. How To Uncover, Heal & Release Painful Life Experiences

7. How to Press Forward & Shift to a Higher Level

8. How To Know God Better & Love Yourself More

Contributing Author in the Following Anthologies and Children's Book:

9. Rhythms of Rest: 40 Devotions for Women on the Move

10. When God Says No: Encouraging Stories of Faith and Accepting the Will of God

11. Words Have Power

My Articles Site:
- Inspired4u@Hubpages

Please leave a book review on Amazon. Thank you for reading and God bless you and yours!

www.ingramcontent.com/pod-product-compliance
Lightning Source LLC
Chambersburg PA
CBHW071428040426
42445CB00012BA/1293